Following

wherever He leads

Joan Crory

with my love,
xx

Ambassador International
Greenville, South Carolina & Belfast, Northern Ireland

www.ambassador-international.com

Following

wherever He leads

Paperback: ISBN: 978-1-62020-197-8

Printed in the UK

Ambassador International
Emerald House
427 Wade Hampton Blvd
Greenville, SC 29609, USA
www.ambassador-international.com

Ambassador Books and Media
The Mount
2 Woodstock Link
Belfast, BT6 8DD, Northern Ireland, UK
www.ambassadormedia.co.uk

Contents

A DIFFERENT STORY

Stories of great Christians tell us about the person they were, what they did and how they lived for God. But all that is in the past and their lives are now finished.

The Gospel story is different. It tells us that Jesus was born, what He did and how He died. But it doesn't stop there; it goes on to tell us that He lives again and that He is still speaking and working now, in our own generation. The way He did things then is often still the way He does things now. And so from all the Gospel stories, we can discover how He works.

Let's take a seemingly unremarkable incident which we read of in Mark 1: 16-18, where Jesus calls two men to be His disciples. What does it have to say to us today? We 're going to ask three questions: Who? What? And How?

WHO?

Jesus sees Simon and Andrew and He calls them to follow

Him. Jesus always calls individuals. He didn't walk along the beach, crying out, "Would anybody like to come and follow Me?" No, out of all the folk who were down at the seaside that day, He singled out these two. Just think back, those of you who are Christians, to your own experience. Maybe other people heard the same sermon but they weren't all converted: God called YOU. Maybe you had brothers and sisters, parents and other relatives but they didn't come to faith the day you did; perhaps they still don't know Him. Think of all the people who live in your street, they're not all Christians, but YOU are! Maybe you never really thought about it like this, that God singled you out from all the others and brought you into His family. Isn't that a wonderful thing!

WHAT?

What did Jesus call them to do? It's interesting to see that He didn't call them to a specific task at this moment. He just said, "Follow Me." It was a call to a personal relationship with Him. This is where some Christians get it so wrong! Some seem to think that following Jesus means doing This and not doing That, being at all the church activities and getting involved. IT'S NOT! First and foremost, it is having a close relationship with Christ day by day. Let's just stop here a moment and ask ourselves, have we got this straight? Is my Christian life a question of what I DO or what I AM? Do I really work at knowing Christ for myself, not merely by listening to sermons or living off other people's experiences? Was He real to me this morning? This is what makes me a Christian, a follower of Jesus.

He called these two brothers to be with Him, to live with Him day by day, to share with Him their joys and their sorrows, their hopes and plans and to sit and listen to Him when He had something He wanted to say to them. If this is how we are following, then everything else in our life will fall into place and we won't just be going through the motions because that's what everybody else is doing.

HOW?

Jesus called them in words they could understand. - he made a sort of fisherman's joke for them – 'I'll make you fishers of men!' They knew what He meant; maybe not all that it would involve but it was clear that He already knew what He wanted them to do for Him.

It's the same with us. Saying, 'I will follow,' isn't the end, it's just the very first step. God called you because He already had a plan for your life, planned even before you were born! Just read Psalm 139 when you have time and you'll see it there. This is where the Christian life can be so exciting. You never know what God has in store. He doesn't reveal our whole life-plan all at once, just one step at a time so that we will learn to trust Him. What you have been doing up to now is not necessarily what He wants you to go on doing for the rest of your life, so keep alert and listen for His voice. He called my husband and me to go to France when we were forty-six and involved in a growing church ministry. So it was Get up and Go, leaving our family and home (and pets!) and discovering an exciting new life. I wouldn't have missed it for the world! The home you live in now may not be where He wants you to stay for ever; have you ever asked Him about that, or are you afraid to do it? It's no good saying, 'I'm too old; I couldn't possibly go somewhere else at the moment'. Where's your foundation for saying that? You all know that old hymn, Trust and Obey. How often have you sung the words?

What He says, we will do, Where He sends, we will go,

Never fear, only Trust and Obey.

That's the attitude we need. Maybe this year, this month, or even as you read this, you will hear God's voice calling you to make a change. He will never ask us to do anything we're not capable of. Paul was quite sure about that. He said, 'He who calls us will also equip us'. We have a God with whom nothing is impossible so let's expect great things from God and attempt great things for Him.

READY AND WILLING

The key thought for today is:

It's not what I can do for God but what God can accomplish through me.

The apostle Paul underlines this thought. He said, in his letter to the Corinthians: 'It is God who works in us, both to will and to do His good pleasure.' It is God who changes our attitudes, in order to make us willing. It is interesting to note that the Bible always portrays people as they are, with all their faults. We are not presented with a host of characters who always do the right thing or have the right attitudes. Let's just think about one or two of them.

Remember Gideon? This young man was working in his threshing floor, hiding from his enemies who were attacking his people. He was scared, but God appeared to him and informed him that he had been chosen to defeat the enemy. Well, Gideon was not only shocked, he was neither willing nor ready to do anything of the sort. Moses was exactly the same. When God spoke to him from the burning bush and told him that he was to lead his people out of slavery in Egypt, he made all sorts of excuses and tried to wriggle out of it. Jeremiah was sent to give God's message to the most unresponsive people and he was painfully conscious of his inadequacy.

So what do we learn from this? Primarily that God chooses unlikely people to do His work. We find this again and again in the biblical narrative. Unlikely and unwilling BUT in every case they ended up doing the job God had given them, in spite of all their hang-ups and doubts. How come? Because God equipped them to do it. And that remains true for us also today. If You feel that God is asking you to do something that really scares you, go ahead anyway, trusting that He will give you the means to do it.

Let's look at some others.

Joseph and Daniel are prime examples of people who remained true to their faith in spite of adverse circumstances. Everything was against them but nothing deterred them from doing what they knew was right and good. Have you ever felt scared to stick up for what you believed or to admit that you were a Christian because of the anti-Christian atmosphere at your work or in your family? I can tell you now that things are going to get worse; we can see the signs already. Learn to be strong now, while things are relatively easy. Someone has said: 'Don't seek to be strong; look to Jesus who makes you strong.' That's good advice.

And then of course there was Ananias who was afraid of the consequences of doing what God asked him to do: Go to Straight Street and deliver a message to Saul of Tarsus, who had been persecuting every Christian he could find!' That was definitely frightening.

The striking thing in all these stories is that although some were unable and some were horribly afraid, yet they all did what was asked of them. Their stories are recorded so that we can learn from them.

Some of my favourites are the ones where what God asked them to do just seemed utterly ridiculous! Poor old Noah, building an enormous boat, miles from the water, taking years to do it and having to endure the constant jeers of the onlookers who thought he'd lost his mind. That's the outstanding example but there are lots of others. Look them up for yourself and you will find that in every instance, folk did what they were told despite the fact that it made no sense to them. That will be a worthwhile study.

But then we come to Philip who was Ready, Willing and Able. He was having a very effective evangelistic campaign in Samaria, and many people were coming into a new relationship with God for the very first time. But God had other plans for Philip and he told him to leave all that exciting success and go out into the desert to meet just one man. And

Philip got up and went, just like that. And the result? – The conversion of a high Ethiopian court official who took the Good News back to Africa.

How often have we sung 'Here I am, wholly available'? But did we really think what we were singing? The tune is nice and the words are great but it's all too easy to sing without giving much thought to the promises we are making to God. Rick Warren, in 'The Purpose-Driven Life' says: You were born by His purpose and for His purpose. That's why we are here, not to live our lives as we please but to show to the world what God is like. Have you ever thought of that? Is that what our neighbours see as we live beside them? Rick Warren again: It is in Christ that we find out who we are and what we are living for.

God does not exist for us; to do what we want or desire. We exist for Him, so that He can work in and through us to achieve His goals. Psalm 139 tells us that He created each of us with a definite plan and purpose in mind. Let's make sure that we discover what that is, and then be Ready and Willing to carry it through.

A BLAMELESS LIFE

In Psalm 101 David declares 'I will give heed to a blameless life,' and another version translates it as, 'I will walk within my house with a perfect heart.' Rather a tall order, I would have thought! But this is David's manifesto; he is setting out for all to see what his aim in life is. He is truly a man after God's own heart. He goes on to touch on every area of his life. He begins with God. Surely that's where we should all start. If our relationship with God is right, then we're on the right track. He starts by recognising who God is and praises Him for His goodness.

Then he moves on and his first priority is his home – sometimes the most difficult place in which to be blameless! Think of Joseph: he was a shining example of someone who, despite all sorts of provocation, lived a life of integrity in his home surroundings. It is a wonderful story of a faithful follower of God who lived a life that in human eyes was really blameless. This is David's aspiration and it should be ours too.

Then, in verse3, David's thoughts move to the community around him; he looks at the sinful world he lives in and he resolves not to get involved in their activities. Daniel is a good example here. In spite of living in a world of idol-worshippers where following God was forbidden, he remained true to what he believed even though he knew he risked death. Even in our world today, in the 21st century, there are Christians facing the very same situation and already hundreds have died for their faith. When we hear of such persecution, it brings reality home to us and with it a challenge as to how would we behave in such a situation. Would our lives be blameless? David's resolution is to stay true to God's standards, no matter what.

The psalm ends with a promise that he will care for God's people. This reminds us of what Jesus said to His disciples: 'By this shall all men know that you are my disciples if you have love one for another'. Can we claim to be blameless in this area too?

In Psalm 119:1-8 we find David back on the same theme again but realising that he needs help to attain his goal. Blamelessness is an impossible goal for us to reach without help. But there's a lovely promise in Colossians 1, that one day we will be able to stand before God, as if we really are blameless, because we will be clothed in the righteousness that Jesus has given us. That doesn't mean we can sit back, do nothing and think we're all right because everything is going to work out in the end. Peter encourages his readers to 'Make every effort to live a pure and blameless life'. We have to play our part. If we are prepared to open our lives fully to God's working, we will experience the blessing that Paul promises to the Thessalonian believers:

> Now may the God of peace make you holy in every way and may your whole spirit and soul and body be kept BLAMELESS until that day when our Lord Jesus Christ comes again.

Let's make that our manifesto.

HINDRANCES TO TOTAL COMMITMENT

We are going to think about three people whose priorities were challenged: The Rich Young Ruler, Martha and Abraham. These are all stories that are very familiar but I want us to accept the challenge they bring.

The Rich Young Ruler.

This was a young man who genuinely wanted to please God. He was doing all the right things and keeping all the rules but he was conscious that something was missing. Does that ring a bell? Jesus put His finger on the one thing necessary: 'Sell all you have....' The hindrance to a full relationship with the Lord in this man's life was his Possessions. There's nothing wrong with Possessions except when they begin to assume too great an importance in life. Here's the challenge: if God asked you to leave your home, or to give up your source of income or to leave your comfortable lifestyle, would you be prepared to do it? If deep down you're thinking 'I couldn't do that- and anyway the Lord will hardly ask me to do that at this stage in my life…' -Beware! He could do just that. That might be the very thing He wants you to do in order to grow closer to Him. If you couldn't do it, you have the same problem as faced this young ruler. He couldn't do it either and the Bible tells us, 'He went away sorrowful.'

Next, let's look at Martha.

What was Martha's hindrance? We have heard it so often – Busyness! But it was busyness in serving the Lord, that can't be wrong, can it? She was consumed with worry over all that she had to do. This is so frequently a trap that Christians fall into. Maybe you're there at this moment? We can be so busy serving God that we squeeze Him out. Sounds crazy but it is sadly true. Martha was doing nothing wrong – and neither was the Rich Young Ruler. In fact in both cases their work was praise-worthy. They both wanted everything done well for the Lord but their relationship with Him was suffering. Are you guilty of this one? Perhaps it would be good to begin to say, 'No' before taking on anything more but rather spend more time with the Lord. It's interesting to note that only three times in the Gospels do we read that Jesus loved someone. And these two people share that honour. Their hindrances didn't cut them off from the Saviour's love, but cut them off from enjoying it.

Lastly we think about Abraham.

Probably one of the most well-known of all the Bible stories and one that really hits home. Abraham's challenge was different from the other two. His relationship with God was good- he was even called 'the friend of God' (Isaiah 41:8). But even he was challenged about his Total Commitment. God asked of him the person dearest to him in all the world. Can you imagine the heartbreak? Think for a moment who that represents for you and put yourself in Abraham's position. And yet it only took him one night to make up his mind!

If God asked us to leave our Possessions for Him, we might struggle, but we could do it. If He asked us to stop doing some of the things we're involved in and where we think we are indispensable, we might regret it and it might be painful. But we could still do it. But this last one? It's a real killer! God's demand couldn't have hurt more. Isaac? Abraham had waited a hundred years for him and loved him with all his heart. Give him up?

Is there someone who sits on the throne of your life, who takes up a great deal of your thoughts and prayers and whom you love more than anyone? God wants him removed from that throne – that's His place! That doesn't mean you stop loving them, of course not but God must have the first place. Our relationship must be all or nothing with Him. We can use the words of a hymn as our prayer:

The dearest idol I have known,
whate'er that idol be,
Help me to tear it from Thy throne
and worship only Thee.

Help us, Lord, to mean these words and to be willing to carry them out in our lives.

BREAKFAST WITH JESUS

After the Resurrection of Jesus, the angels give a message to the women who had come to the tomb: 'Say to His disciples, Jesus will meet with you in Galilee'.

In the story in John 21, we find seven disciples. And where are they? -On the shores of Lake Galilee. What more likely place to meet Jesus again? He had done so much of His teaching here and it was here that Peter and Andrew, James and John had heard His call to follow Him.

They were waiting for Jesus to come to them but Peter, impetuous Peter, couldn't just sit around doing nothing while he waited and he decides to go fishing. The others go with him and they are out all night but in vain, they return to shore with empty nets.

As the day dawns and they are nearing the shore, they see a figure on the beach. He calls out and asks them the question they would have preferred not to answer: 'Have you caught anything?' and they have to admit that they haven't. Then amazingly they hear these words of advice in v.6, 'Cast your net on the right side of the boat and you'll get a good catch.' Now these were seasoned, professional fishermen. Why on earth would casting their net on the other side of the boat make any difference? It was the same water and the same method… but amazingly, they obey- and witness a miracle!

At this point it dawns on John who the stranger is and he exclaims; 'It is the Lord!' Peter, on hearing that, jumps straight into the water to get to Jesus. When they finally get to the beach they see that Jesus already has fish; they're already cooking on the fire but He invites them to make a contribution. And they start their new day having breakfast with the risen Lord.

A simple story that is familiar to us all but there are some profound lessons we can learn from it:

Firstly: When God asks us to wait, there is no need to be idle. Do what lies at hand. When His time comes, He will direct us.

Secondly: On our own, without Jesus, we can achieve nothing even though we might appear to others to be experts.

Thirdly: With Him, nothing is impossible. We may think we know how to do something but God may have a different way and we need to listen to Him.

Forthly: Obedience always brings blessing. Suppose they

hadn't obeyed... they could have insisted that they knew what they were doing and His suggestion didn't make sense. What they would have missed!

Next: God doesn't need us! Jesus already had fish but he chose to involve His friends. God doesn't really need us to do His work, but He chooses to include us in what He is doing, if only we are willing. Paul talks about working 'in partnership' with God.

Lastly: starting the day with God is the recipe for a successful life. It is so important that we take time with Him each day to enjoy His presence and to listen to what He is saying.

Is that what you do? If not, make a resolution to have breakfast with Jesus. It will be the best start to each day.

WE WOULD SEE JESUS

I wonder if you have ever thought how much easier it would be to live a life that is pleasing to God if you had actually seen Jesus? We will look at several people in the Bible who, at some stage in their life, saw the Lord and the difference it made to them.

In Acts 9:1-6 we read about Paul. At the time of this story, he was still called Saul and was hell-bent on destroying any followers of Jesus that he could find, hauling them off to prison and, by doing so, becoming a fierce enemy of the newly-hatched church. It was during a journey to Damascus that he encountered Jesus for real. He had heard a great deal about Him, had even contributed to the killing of Stephen, the first Christian martyr but now he sees Him face to face. Note that it was while he was opposed to all He stood for that Jesus revealed Himself to Paul and it turned his life from Opposition to Self-Sacrificing Service for the rest of his life. His whole outlook was completely changed. This is how the Christian life begins for all of us, with a complete change-around of our attitudes and behaviour.

But our need to see the Lord clearly doesn't end with our conversion, that's just our first 'sight' of Him. Let's have a look at some people who already knew the Lord but still needed a special encounter with Him.

John 20:26-29 tells us about Thomas. Now he was one of the chosen twelve who lived and worked with Jesus for years. He'd been a witness to some amazing miracles and heard some revolutionary teaching. Is this like you? Maybe you have been a Christian for years but there are still times when you go through times of doubt and unbelief, just like Thomas. He hadn't been there when Jesus had appeared to all the other disciples and he was just disillusioned by His death. He was feeling a bit alienated from his friends and really miserable in his unbelief and that was when Jesus appeared right in front of him! Faced with His reality, what effect did this have on Thomas? – His Doubt was transformed into complete Trust and Worship.

In the Old Testament, in 1 Kings 19, we can read about Elijah. He was a prophet, well-known as a Man of God and yet he is in deep depression, wondering if there was any point in continuing to stand out for God. Have you ever felt like that? This is something which specially affects those in any sort of Christian leadership, I feel, but it can happen to us all. It was when Elijah was on the point of giving up altogether that God stepped in. It was then that Depression turned to Re-Commission and a recovery of his zeal.

Next we turn to Job. Job saw God in his distress. Did anyone ever suffer such a catalogue of misfortune as poor Job! He was sick in body and mind, given nothing but useless platitudes by his friends, told to rebel by his wife and getting no answers from God. It was an awful time for him and his distress was real and painful. In the end, he fires questions at God, demanding answers but he doesn't get them. Instead God reveals Himself to Job in such a powerful way that his questions become irrelevant and no longer matter. His distress was turned to Awe and Worship.

What about Mary Magdalene? We see her, in John 20, coming to the tomb where Jesus was buried, heartbroken, mourning the loss of her dearest Friend. She felt completely lost and didn't know how she was going to cope. But then she lifted her eyes – and saw the Lord Jesus! What a beautiful story this is! Her Sorrow was turned into Rejoicing.

Lastly we will take a quick look at Isaiah. In chapter 6, we find him engaged in Service for God. He was going about his duties faithfully, doing all the things he had to do, not expecting God to suddenly reveal Himself but he was in the right place at the right time and without warning he 'saw the Lord'. For him, his routine Service took on a whole new Direction.

None of these people had the same experience and there are no hard-and-fast rules to follow but surely we all long for an experience like these; to look back on when life gets difficult and which would revitalise our lives in God's service. There are two verses which should encourage us. We're not ever going to see Jesus in the flesh but there are times when we will 'see' God.

'Be still and know that I am God.' It can be in our times of quiet as we think about something in our daily Bible reading or as we are just talking to God, that suddenly He will reveal Himself to us in a new way. The promise is: 'You will seek Me and you will find Me when you search for me with all your heart.'

THE HURT OF INJUSTICE

There is nothing so painful as unjust accusation, whether from a colleague, a partner or a friend but particularly if it comes from a fellow Christian. So how do we cope? – Not with retaliation!

What we have to learn to do is to throw ourselves on God after having made sure that there is no truth in the allegation. After all, God knows our hearts and He knows the truth of the situation better than we do ourselves.

If we turn to the Bible, we will find lots of passages which refer to this very situation. We find examples of people who have suffered the deep wounds of criticism and rejection from those for whom they had spent time, effort and care.

Take Moses, for example. He had reluctantly taken on the immense task of leading God's people out of Egypt, away from slavery under Pharaoh. He hadn't wanted to do it in the first place but because God had called him and promised to be with him, he had obeyed. But what happened? As a result of his demanding that Pharaoh set the people free, their job had been made twice as hard and their slavery even more bitter. And naturally, the people hated him for it. But it wasn't his fault, he was only trying to help. INJUSTICE! How does he cope with the situation? He complains bitterly, but not to his friends or to his brother Aaron; he goes straight to God. And God promises that He has the situation in hand and that He will fulfil His promise to rescue His people in the end.

What about the apostle Paul? He experienced the same problems, only worse. His problems were in the churches. He had all sorts of things said about him and criticism spread about him. But his response was that he did not take these things to heart; he was content, after searching his own heart, to leave the outcome with God, the ultimate just judge. Constantly in his letters to the church at Corinth, he insists 'but we do not lose heart'. He didn't allow hurtful words to totally discourage him or cause him to give up on the task God had entrusted to him. How was he able to be so strong? Surely it stemmed from his utter trust in God, knowing that what he was doing was what God had asked him to do, come what may.

He was not afraid to defend himself if the opportunity presented itself, but it was always in a humble spirit with no hint of resentment or retaliation confident that God knew the truth. That doesn't mean he didn't feel hurt; he is often sad about what is going on but that doesn't deflect him from his task.

Of course, our supreme example is Jesus Himself. If anyone was ever hurt and rejected by those He loved, it was Him. Let down by his nearest disciples, who forsook him and fled when danger loomed; having one of his closest friends denying that he even knew Him, betrayed to His enemies by one of His inner circle. Even His own family thought he was mad! That's pretty shattering and remember He was totally human, as well as totally God, so He felt it all deeply. But we know that He never retaliated, never answered back, went on loving those who let Him down, never employed angry words. And Paul says 'Let this mind be in you which was also in Christ Jesus'. In other words, that's what we have to strive for, to be like Him in our reactions to people who hurt us. That is far from easy but it is the only way to keep our hearts at peace with ourselves and with each other.

Oswald Chambers says, 'Don't seek to be strong; seek to be united with Jesus who makes us strong.'

A LESSON IN PRAYING

The Bible is full of teaching about Prayer and all Christians agree that it is vital, but so many of us struggle with it. Do we subconsciously feel that prayer is an excuse for not doing anything? If so, we've got the wrong idea! Prayer is the real work and the ensuing activity should be just reaping the benefits of the praying.

If we are serious about our walk with Jesus, we should be involved in praying for others, for what we see on the TV and hear on the radio, for the events in our church and in our world, as well as for ourselves. 'Intercession' is a triangle: one person going to another on behalf of a third.

Ronald Dunn, in his book *'Don't Just Stand There, PRAY Something!'* describes prayer as 'bold, daring and audacious'. Does that sound like your prayer times? In Luke 11, we have the story of a man who goes to his friend for help. His situation called for Boldness; he went at midnight! Not a convenient time to go knocking on someone's door, even a good friend. And the answer has been translated as 'My children are packed around me in bed' but even that does not deter the caller.

Look at how Abraham spoke with God when Sodom was about to be destroyed because of the wickedness in the city. He kept on and on, bargaining with God that He might save it if there were fifty righteous people found there, or forty-five…or forty…, thirty… and so on until he arrived at ten. Now, if that isn't bold, I don't know what is!

Moses had the same temerity. While Moses was up in the mountain getting the Ten Commandments, the people down in the valley got tired of waiting for him and built a golden calf and were worshipping it. God's anger was fierce against them but Moses dared to challenge Him in such a way that He didn't carry out their punishment. That took courage!

The result of these daring prayers? God relented. Does God change His mind? We don't understand. Does prayer change God's plans? Vance Havner says: 'I don't understand how electricity works, But I'm not going to sit around in the dark until I do!' We do know that there are things God will do in answer to prayer that He might not do if we don't pray.

The next thing we need to be an effective pray-er is Persistence. In the story of the two friends, the friend had no intention of getting up to help. So what changed his mind? The man in need was persistent – the word can also mean 'shameless'. He wasn't concerned about anything except the needs of the traveller who had arrived at his house. Jesus told another story, about a woman who begs a judge for help and keeps on asking until she gets it. Jesus commends the 'continual coming' of the woman. Do we get discouraged when we seem to get no answer when we pray? Do we give up too easily?

Remember the story of Jacob who wrestled with the angel? His plea was, 'I won't let you go until you bless me.' Of course the angel could have left at any time. Was he waiting to see if Jacob seriously wanted what he was asking for?

Praying is often hard work. If your Christianity is comfortable and easy and doesn't disturb your life in any way, you might not even be aware of the battle that is raging.

The man in the first story was Desperate. He says, 'A caller has come to ME, not to anyone else, he needs MY help'. There are people who have come to us, neighbours, colleagues at work, people we meet, our family members. They are our inescapable responsibility. You may think that you are in your present situation by chance but you're not. The early Christians were 'scattered abroad' through persecution. It was God's intended scattering of the seed, to bring life to the whole world. And God has put you where you are to help meet the needs of the folk around you.

The first man says, 'I have nothing to set before him.' Is this your problem? People all around us have needs, and we have nothing to set before them. Is that why we shrink at the words 'witness, testimony, outreach' etc.? Is that why we're very happy to leave that sort of thing to the pastor or the official evangelist or to the 'keener' members of the church?

In the end, the friend agrees to get out of bed and give him as much bread as he needed. We have nothing to give but our Heavenly Father has a store of 'bread' and He will give us even more than we need if we are prepared to pray with boldness, persistence and desperation.

IT'S NO JOKE!

How often do we say that! Lose the car keys, slogging to the shops in the pouring rain, cleaning up after the children etc. etc. 'NO JOKE!'

It's clearly No Joke. But have you ever thought we could say that about our Christian life? Think of some of the Christians we have all heard about. There's Joni – paralysed in a swimming accident at 17, confined to a wheelchair, unable to do her own hair or clean her own teeth for the rest of her life. That's no joke. Or Jim Elliott and his friends – taking the gospel to the Auca Indians of the jungle in South America, and speared to death on the banks of the river as they tried to share God's love. That's definitely no joke. What about the martyrs who were burnt at the stake? Perhaps even more shockingly to us because it's happening in our own time – Christians being crucified and beheaded for no other reason than that they are followers of Christ.

The Christian life is not an easy option for the weak and fainthearted. It requires courage and perseverance. The Bible warns us to be prepared for battle, to take up our cross and to deny ourselves. That means give up all rights and hand our lives completely over to God, whatever may happen.

Jesus said some strange things: rejoice when you are persecuted! The world will hate you, but remember it hated Me first!

Does this sound like your experience?

Why bother, people might ask. Why choose such a difficult path?

The answer is, because of the blessing it brings.

Obedience ALWAYS brings blessing.

So what is there to encourage us to live a sacrificial life? There's Security. We know that if God is in control, nothing will happen to us by accident or without Him knowing. There is Guidance; the thrill of seeing that He had a path laid out before us. There's a Worldwide Family that we belong to. Wherever in the world we go, we recognise easily other members of this family, even if we can't speak their language. It's an amazing experience. There is the Confidence of being sure that we have been forgiven for sins past and present and that one day we will be presented to God, faultless. That's surely worth knowing.

If we weigh up the pros and cons, there is really no contest.

Jim Elliott famously said,

He is no fool who gives what he cannot keep to gain what he cannot lose.

How true that is! So don't be a fool.

OUR CHANGING ROLES

Have you ever stopped to think how often your role in life has changed? Many changes come in the normal course of events, and as such we accept them more or less without much problem.

It is the natural order of things: from schoolgirl to working woman; from single girl to fiancée, wife, mother. We accept these roles for better, for worse, for richer, for poorer and work them out with a greater or lesser degree of anticipation and joy. Of course they bring us problems and heartaches from time to time and in this modern world attacks on family life are increasing from day to day. We need to return again and again to God's Word and the encouragement of such words as: 'If any of you lacks wisdom, let him ask of God.'

But there are other role changes which come to us, not in the natural order of things but which are thrust upon us by unforeseen circumstances, or as a result of other people's decisions, or indeed by a positive choice on our part. It is these changes which can bring with them unimagined trauma and can cause our faith to waver. All change brings insecurity to a greater or lesser degree and often our heart's cry will be, 'O Thou who changes not, abide with me!' Let's consider the role change which comes from our voluntary choice. Maybe this is where you find yourself at this moment. You feel that the Lord is prompting you to offer yourself for some new service for Him. You are sure you should say, 'Yes,' but you are scared of not being up to the job, of not being capable to see it through. Paul assures us, in Corinthians, that our capability comes from God. That doesn't mean it will be either easy or straight forward but it does mean that God will equip us to do it. Relying on Him when we know we can't do it on our own will result in a strengthening of our faith as we prove that his strength is made perfect in our weakness.

I read a story of a man who offered to take a Bible Class for teenage boys. After a week or two, he was ready to give up; the boys were inattentive and badly behaved and he felt he was wasting his time. On one occasion, having reached the end of his tether, he sent up this heartfelt prayer: 'O God, give me Your patience to deal with these lads, for mine has just about run out!' I like the wisdom of that prayer. Do not struggle on in your new role trying vainly to cope in your own strength. Remember it is when we are feeling really weak that the Lord will step in and help. So ask Him!

Perhaps for some of us there have been – or will be – even more dramatic changes. A parent becomes ill and we have to give up work, stay at home and become a 'carer'; or suddenly it is redundancy and from being a wage-earner overnight we become one of the great unemployed; illness hits us or perhaps a serious accident and from being an active person we have to accept the role of an invalid ... the possibilities are endless and frightening. How do we cope when this sort of role-change hits us?

Oswald Chambers says that when upheavals occur in our lives, we must say, 'Lord, how am I to react to this? How do You want me to react?' That is all very well but, being human, we find that often we react negatively almost before we have time to turn to God. 'It's not fair!' 'God, why does it have to be me?' 'I can't bear it!' etc. Even Job had his problems and asked Why? But the Holy Spirit is at work in us and He will eventually bring us to the point where we will have to say, 'Lord, not my will, but Yours.' It will no doubt be a very painful process – (Have you read the book *'Joni'*?) - but for the true child of God there can be no other solution. It is a test of trusting.

How easily we say, when life is simple, 'I trust God to work out His plan for my life' but God may call our bluff and let us learn just what it means to really put our lives completely under His control. No, He is not vindictive in doing so, He tenderly wants to teach us the serenity that comes from finding all that we need in Him. How often do we read in the Psalms, 'God is my Rock, my Refuge, my strong Tower.' David also said, 'My times are in Your hands'. In other words, 'Lord, I trust myself and my circumstances totally to You.' Can you honestly say that even when life is at its blackest? That is what being a Christian is all about: living closely with God through thick and thin and learning the truth of His promise that His grace is enough to meet all our needs.

DECISIONS, DECISIONS!

Life is full of decisions, isn't it? We make them every day, all day. There are the easy ones: Shall I have tea or coffee at breakfast? What shall I wear today? What shall I make for the meal tonight?

When we are growing up, there are the BIG decisions. Shall I marry him (or her)? What career shall I choose? When shall I leave home? These are life-changing choices and can cause us anxious moments or sleepless nights.

As we get older, the sort of decisions we have to make tend to change a bit and sometimes we put them off: Should I go to the doctor about this pain? Dare I go to my neighbour and tell him what his teenagers are up to, or dare I go and confront those children about their anti-social behaviour? Some of these can have dire consequences which is why we hesitate to make them.

But important as some of these are, there are some that

are even more serious. Jesus had something to say on this subject and we are going to look at two stories He told about people who made decisions, rightly or wrongly. The first story is found in Matthew 21. It is very short but teaches us an important lesson. Maybe you will recognise yourself in this story...

A father has two sons. He says to the first, 'Son, go and work today in the vineyard.' A simple request, but the son refuses point blank and says he won't go. So the father asked the other son and he replies, 'Of course I'll go!' What a contrast! But that's not the end of the story. The son who had refused, later thinks better of it and goes and puts in a good day's work in the vineyard. The other son who seemed so willing and obedient didn't go after all. Now, what can we learn from this simple little story? I think we all fall into one or other of these categories. Maybe you are like the first boy. You have heard God speaking to you at some time and you knew you should respond but you didn't do it. This went on, perhaps for a long time but in the end you realised that the only thing you could do was to be obedient to God's call. You asked for His forgiveness and received Christ into your life. That's good.

But perhaps that doesn't fit you? Perhaps you are more like the other son; outwardly you seem to be doing all the right things, you go to church, you have respect for God, maybe you even pray and give your money in to church but deep inside your heart, you're not really a Christian at all.

You have never obeyed God's call and you are not part of God's family. Other people may think you are but God knows the truth, and so do you. This could be the most important decision of your life and you need to make it.

Story number two is found in Matthew 25. Now, this one is specially for those of us who are Christians and who want to serve the Lord with our lives. A master, going on a journey, calls his servants and entrusts to each one a certain amount of money which he must put to good use before his master returns. One man got five silver coins, another got two and the third got just one. Each one was responsible to work with the amount he was given and was to give an account to the master on his return.

Let's note certain things; firstly, they were not all given the same amount. God has given to each one of us certain gifts and talents and we're not all equally gifted. To some people this is a problem. They look at others who they see as more talented and they envy them. But listen, it's not how many talents we have that's important – it's what we do with what we've got! God will not hold us responsible for what other people do. Secondly, God never demands from us abilities that we do not possess. Trying to serve where we're not gifted is like putting a square peg into a round hole. The bible says, 'To him (her) who knows how to do good, and doesn't do it, to him that is sin.' That's serious. We may not be equal in talent but we should be equal in effort and willingness. How do you respond when you are asked to do something for the

Lord? Do you usually say, 'No' not because you can't do it but perhaps you are scared to try? Remember, Obedience always brings Blessing.

The master returned and called his servants to account. Each of the first two had made a real effort and increased the money given to them. They were both equally commended and their master was pleased. But the third man had done nothing with what he had been given. He had hidden it and it was no better than when he had received it. He was in disgrace and felt his master's displeasure. Why was he punished? Because he did not even try! He didn't lose his talent; he just didn't use it. Do you get the picture? The more we use our talents, the more they will improve. Look at the example of a musician or an athlete: the more he practises, the better he gets. If that is true on the physical plane, how much more is it true on the spiritual. Shouldn't our highest aim be to hear Him say, 'Well done, good and faithful servant!'

Have either of these stories made you feel a bit uncomfortable? Please take a moment today to look at your life. There are decisions to be made.

GOOD HEALTH

Over recent years, as a nation we have become increasingly health conscious. Every magazine has a Slimmer's Guide or programme, and sheets of exercises to give us a good figure, or for men, a nice 'six-pack'! We all get caught up in it; we say to our children 'Don't eat that, it'll give you spots/destroy your teeth/make you fat'. We're constantly being warned not to eat certain foods because of the harm they can do to our bodies.

And what about exercise? The jogging craze, Keep Fit and Aerobics are on the go in church halls and leisure centres in every town.

Why? Because people are beginning to realise that Good Health is one of the most precious gifts we have. God created us body, mind and spirit and we need to be healthy in all three realms.

Let's think first about our Physical Health. In Proverbs 3 we find promises, not of wealth but of well-being. Look at verses 2, 8 and 10. Solomon talks about long life and peace, about health to our bodies and material prosperity. Aren't these the things we all want in our lives?

What about Mental Health? As I write there is a discussion ongoing in Parliament about the shortness of funds in this area and an increasing problem, especially among our young people. Something is sadly wrong here. How many folks are taking Librium and Valium and all sorts of anti-depressants? Why is such a large proportion of our population living on drugs? This applies both to Christians and non-Christians. Our minds are troubled. Maybe we call it 'nerves' but we will all probably suffer from it at some point in our lives. I had two very frightening years of it and it is not a time I would wish to repeat! If you have never had mental problems, praise the Lord for that and live closely to Him. Depression, at its height is a clinical condition which is crying out for help. Certainly God has given doctors wisdom to deal with it and there is no shame in admitting that you have a real problem.

One cause of depression can be Fear. These days there is a real dread of persecution because of our faith. It seems that our nation is moving further and further away from being God-fearing and already many Christians have paid the price for their faith. But there are other causes too: Fear for our future, fear of illness, fear for wayward children – and the list goes on. There's a lovely verse in Isaiah 26:3.

'You will keep in perfect peace all who trust in you, all whose thoughts are fixed on You.'

If we could only grasp the truth of this, it could prevent a great deal of the anxiety and worry that we live with. Peter, Jesus' impulsive friend, had learned this truth and we are told that he was sleeping peacefully in prison on the eve of his execution!

Then we need to think about our Spiritual Health. Even the most ungodly folk today are aware of the Supernatural. There's Transcendental Meditation, Yoga, New Age, astrologers and fortune -tellers and séances. Some young people are dabbling in the occult, and how many read their 'stars' every day? Somehow we are born with 'eternity in our hearts' and with a realisation that there is more than just a physical existence. People may not recognise this as an awareness of God, but that's basically what it is. Blaise Pascal said once, 'Our hearts are restless until they find their rest in Thee.' That's the truth. The Bible teaches that we can be totally sure of our spiritual well-being, without turning to all these things, and that our future is secure in God's hands. Isaiah affirmed: 'I will trust and not be afraid'. Isn't that the way we want to be too? If our lives are in a right relationship with God, not only will we be Spiritually Healthy but our Physical and Mental state will improve as well. It doesn't come to us automatically; it needs to be worked at. But if you are serious about it, you'll find that it works.

BLESSED ARE THE PEACEMAKERS

Life is full of conflict, one way and another, everywhere we turn. Television series are filled with warring families, broken relationship and violence. The trouble is that it is not found just on the television but we find it all around us.

Thomas Watson said: 'Satan kindles the fire of contention in men's hearts and then warms himself at the fire.' Sadly, true.

It is even found in the church. We hear of factions and splits among church people and churches being divided. But, as Solomon said, 'There is nothing new under the sun' – we find it happening in Bible times. Paul wrote in one of his letters about a pair of ladies in the church who just couldn't get on with each other. They were called Euodias and Syntyche. The problem was that their personal falling-out was affecting the unity of the church. And it needed to be dealt with speedily before it caused real harm. Conflict needs to be addressed as soon as it becomes apparent. Small resentments which are left unresolved can very easily grow into mountains of discord.

Most of us dislike confrontation but avoiding trouble doesn't remove the problem, it just postpones the inevitable. If you are conscious of something coming between you and another person in your church, don't wait for them to come and apologise to you, even if you are convinced that they are in the wrong. Jesus told His followers that if they found themselves in such a situation that they were to be the ones to make the first move. It's no good feeling that your rights have been violated, that's not the issue. The issue is God's standard: 'As much as is possible, live at peace with everyone.' Stop and think about how Jesus behaved; did He stand up for His rights? No, He didn't. In spite of all the unjust accusations thrown at Him, He kept His mouth shut and didn't retaliate.

Do we look for revenge when we feel we've been wronged? Do we have a need to retaliate? Think again. That's not God's way. 'Revenge is sweet' we're told but it's not. If you are a true follower of Jesus, you have to show to the world what He is like, and that means Forgiveness. Forgiveness is liberating. Forgive freely and openly, and you will find that you have real peace in your heart. God's peace.

Peter's advice is, 'Seek peace and pursue it.' We have to seek it. It's not necessarily the obvious way to go but if we choose to search for it, it will bring blessing not just to us but to others too. It is advice worth following. So if you are in a conflict situation, whether great or small, do all you can to resolve it quickly, even if it might mean eating 'humble pie'!

GET THINGS RIGHT!

I wonder if, as you have read the Gospels, you have ever noticed that Jesus saw things totally differently from the way we see them?

Let's take the story of the Feeding of the Five Thousand. The day was drawing to a close and there were all these people still hanging about hoping that Jesus would start talking again or perform a miracle or two. You and I would probably have agreed with the disciples' solution to the problem – 'Lord, Send them away! This is too big a problem for us to deal with.' But Jesus' solution was exactly the opposite – 'You feed them!'

Such an idea was far beyond the disciples' imaginings BUT what a glorious outcome when they obeyed! With two little fish and five small bread rolls, five thousand people had more than enough to eat.

Long years before, God had stated, 'My thoughts are not your thoughts, neither are My ways your ways.' And these followers of Jesus had just proved the truth of that.

In Luke 10, we meet another situation, showing us clearly two vastly differing attitudes. Here we are in the home at Bethany where Mary, Martha and Lazarus lived. They were a family that Jesus truly loved and they loved Him. Martha had a reputation as a hostess to hold up and she was doing her very best to serve up something special for her Friend. Remember this poem? –

If Jesus came to your house to spend a day or two,

If He came unexpectedly, I wonder what you'd do?

Oh, I know you'd give your nicest room to such an honoured guest,

And all the food you'd serve to Him would be the very best...

That was Martha. She was doing her very best to please her guest but she was just getting stressed over it. She was busy and flustered and it annoyed her intensely that while she was working away in the kitchen, and incidentally missing all that Jesus was saying, Mary was sitting there, enjoying His presence doing absolutely nothing to help.

Her solution was – Make Mary see things MY way. Make her come and give me a hand.

Jesus saw it differently: Martha, you need to see things My way!

Some of the things that get us stressed are not important

to Jesus. We can become consumed by what we are doing not realising that the value of our work springs from the time we spend with Him.

What Martha was doing, she was doing for Jesus, but did she feel blessed and fulfilled in her work? No, she was frustrated and filled with thoughts of herself and self-pity was creeping in. Not only that, but deep down she knew she was missing out.

Don't develop a ministry instead of a relationship. Your Christian service will become nothing but a chore and you will find your heart growing empty and discontented. Nobody should be so busy working for the Kingdom that they have no time for the King!

Can you see yourself here? Developing any relationship needs to be worked at. Have you ever noticed how often, when you have settled down to have time with God, you keep thinking of all the things that need to be done that day?

Mary was part of the group around Jesus and Martha wanted to call her away, quite legitimately, she reckoned. There will always be people who will call us away from our Quiet Time, from the Prayer Meeting, from learning more from God's Word; maybe family, or neighbours or even other Christians. Be alert!

Busyness cannot rob us of our walk with Jesus but it can reduce the quality. But just a thought about people who are not busy; people who are ill or old or just retired with lots of time on their hands. Is that time used to get to know Jesus more and more each day, or is it used to watch lots more TV, or to spend more time in bed or play golf five times a week? There's nothing essentially wrong with any of those things but, looking at the way you spend your life would the Lord have to say to you as He did to Martha: 'One thing is needed; come and spend more time with Me.'

THE STEPS OF OBEDIENCE

In Luke chapter 5, we find a story that gives us a clear insight into how Jesus works in the life of an individual.

Here we have the usual crowd of people following Jesus, hanging on His every word, listening to His teaching. But who does Jesus turn His attention to? In verse 2 we are told, that He turns to a couple of fishermen. Really they were the most unlikely people, because to all intents and purposes, they weren't even listening to Him; they were sitting on the beach, boats pulled up beside them, attending to their fishing nets. They were busily preparing for their night's work.

If we had been choosing someone to be involved in the Lord's work that day, who would we have picked? – One of the front row of the crowd, no doubt, someone who was showing obvious interest. But that wasn't how Jesus thought.

Have you ever thought that you are an unlikely choice for the Lord to use? You've no obvious talents, you can't stand up and speak in front of people, you don't think you're very clever... Watch out! God can and will use you. Jesus invests in unlikely individuals. The fishermen were described by the religious leaders as 'unlearned and ignorant men'!

Peter was one of these men and there were three steps in his obedience:

Step 1:

Jesus asked for a loan of the boat. That wasn't very difficult but if Peter had refused he wouldn't have experienced the steps of deeper obedience which lay ahead. It didn't cost him anything this time and it was an easy thing to do.

This is where we must begin. Maybe the Lord has whispered in your ear that you could use your car to give someone a lift to church, to take children to their Children's Club or to lift the phone and ring someone you know is having problems, or just to ask a neighbour in for coffee – and you haven't done it. Maybe you're waiting for Him to ask you to do something more special and then you will obey? Do you remember the story of Naaman? You can read it in 2Kings 5. If he hadn't done the simple thing he was told to do, he would have missed the greatest blessing of his life. It's the same with us. God will not entrust us with great tasks if we can't obey Him in the little things.

Step 2:

In verse 3, Jesus enlists Peter's help to push the boat out

away from the shore. This was a bit more inconvenient. It interrupted his life's routine but once again, he obeyed.

Step 3:

This led on to deeper involvement. Peter had been a fisherman all his life and he knew the best conditions for netting a good catch. But here is Jesus – and what did He know about fishing? – telling him to go out into the lake and let his nets down. That just seemed daft; middle of the day, sun shining, not a good time for fishing. Peter did gently suggest that perhaps that wasn't such a good idea but he added a very important rider; 'If you say so…' That is the key. This is where trust comes in when we say, 'I'll trust where I cannot see, Lord.'

God will take us from simple obedience to something more difficult. And the result? For Peter, it was a really good catch, his net was full to overflowing. But it wasn't a blessing just for him, James and John, his fishermen colleagues shared in it too. Through our obedience, God's blessing can overflow to others.

What else? Peter gained a new insight into who Jesus was! And lastly, it led Peter into much greater service. The story ends with him leaving his fishing boat and, with James and John, giving up his way of life to start a new life as a follower of the Lord.

At the beginning of this story, Peter had no idea of the radical change that was about to come into his life. And as we learn each day to increase our trust in God, we have no idea where he may lead us. We have only to obey each whisper of His voice and who knows what changes could result from our obedience. The Christian life is far from dull; it can become really exciting if we make up our minds to do things God's way and not ours.

THE BIG ISSUE

You are a Christian. Maybe you have been one for many years but for some reason there seems to be something missing. The joy that is supposed to be an intrinsic element of your Christian life just isn't there – it seems to have passed you by. Don't think you are the only one who feels like this. Years ago, AWTozer called it the 'missing jewel' of Christian experience.

The thing is, you seem to be doing everything right but something vital is not there. Can I suggest a possible solution to your problem? Perhaps it's a matter of the Big Issue. To face this, you need to be absolutely honest with yourself: Is there an issue in your life that you are constantly aware of? Perhaps it is an issue that God has spoken to you about before; something that occupies your thoughts every day and even takes up some of your prayer-time. It might be a relationship that is very close to your heart or a habit that you have never been able to break.

That still small voice you hear now and then saying, 'You

need to sort this out', gets pushed to the back of your mind and you continue as normal. Could that be the reason that deep down you know it is coming between you and God but basically you are not willing to change. I am fairly sure that no-one else knows anything about it; it's something precious to you that you don't want to relinquish even though you are aware that it is getting in the way of your spiritual growth. I wrote a poem a few years ago for someone who was exactly in this position. Read it and see if it covers what is going on in your heart too.

If God has shown you that this issue has taken first place in your life, in your thoughts, in your affections, then you have to realise that it is taking the place that should rightly be His and what you have to do is to de-throne it. That doesn't mean you end the relationship, if that's what it is, you just put it in its proper place. The habit might need to go altogether or just to be regulated to less time and thought. You know yourself what it must entail. And don't imagine the process won't be painful, it will. But if you are honestly want to be right with the Lord, you have to offer up this Big Issue in your life as a sacrifice to God, give it to Him and let Him deal with it.

This is the only way to regain any peace of heart and mind: Seek FIRST the Kingdom of God, and he has promised that he will meet all your needs. It's something that has to be done, so make up your mind to do it and do it soon. That's the way to blessing.

The Battle is the Lord's

Lord, You have put Your finger on
The one thing I must do
If I'm to know the peace and joy
Of fellowship with You.
But, oh it's hard to win the fight –
The battle rages long
But though I know my flesh is weak,
Praise God, I know He's strong.
It's He who wins the victory,
The power is in His hand
And when I fear my strength will fail,
I know He'll understand.
I know that I must learn to trust
Completely in His power –
Believe Him when He says, 'Fear not,
I'm with you every hour.'
I know that on my own I'll fall
But Christ my Lord is near.
He is the King Omnipotent,
So what have I to fear?

THIS THING IS FROM ME

I wonder do you find yourself in a difficult or hurtful situation today? There are so many things that can, and do, go wrong in life, I wonder how do you react? As Christians our reaction should be different from that of the folk around us who have no conception of God at work in their lives.

Let's keep this thought at the forefront of our minds when troubles arrive. – God is saying, 'This thing is from Me.' It will give us a spiritual perspective on our circumstances if we can see God's hand in them.

Perhaps you have financial difficulties today: business failure, loss of employment or just the daily struggle to live on your pension. What does the Lord say to us? - Seek first the kingdom of God and all these things will be added to us.

'All these things' means everything we need for our basic daily life. Perhaps we have to learn to make do with less? In that case, let's make our aim to be like Paul who had learned to be content in whatsoever state he found himself.

Note, it was something he had to learn, it didn't come without effort. But he was convinced of one thing; that God would supply his every need. (Phil.4:19)

Maybe you're hurting because your friends have let you down? That can be a very painful experience. But the Lord Jesus knows exactly how you feel. Remember what happened to Him? -One of His 'set' betrayed Him, one of His closest friends swore that he didn't even know Him and when He was arrested and needed His friends' loving support, what happened? Every one of them ran off and left Him! Tell Him all about your hurt and discover that He is always faithful.

Perhaps your plans to serve Him have all gone wrong? Is that because they were perhaps your own ideas, formulated by you, with the best intentions no doubt, but without consulting Him first? Or did other people get in the way of their fulfilment and you find yourself disappointed? Don't worry, God wants to tell you His projects, suited to your capabilities, with your good in mind, your joy and His glory. Ask Him to show them to you. He has 'plans to prosper you and not to harm you, to give you a future and a hope'. (Jer.29:11)

But your problem may not be any of these. Is it physical suffering of some sort, the weariness of constant pain? Let God be your comfort. The Bible is full of lovely promises for you. Jesus Himself said, 'Come to Me, all you who are weary and heavy-laden and I will give you rest'. The Bible encourages us to cast all our cares and worried on God because He cares for us. He knows our situation and even in broken health our spirits can be set free if we put our complete trust in Him.

There's a lovely verse in Isaiah: 'They that wait upon the Lord shall renew their strength. They shall mount up with wings like eagles, they shall run and not faint.' What a lovely prospect! Freedom, Liberty, the ability to soar up above our problems with a liberated spirit, trusting in God to make us 'more than conquerors'. We can be victorious even in the most difficult circumstances.

Just remember, if 'This Thing' is from God, He's right there in it with us and with His help we can overcome.

MEMORANDUM

To: Jesus of Nazareth, Woodcrafter Carpenter's Shop, Nazareth

From: Jordan Management Consultants, Jerusalem.

Dear Sir,

Thank you for submitting the resumes of the twelve men you have picked for management positions in your new organisation. All of them have now taken our battery of tests; we have not only run the results through our computer but also arranged personal interviews for each of them with our psychologist and vocational aptitude consultant.

It is the staff opinion that most of your nominees are lacking in background, educational and vocational aptitude for the type of enterprise you are undertaking. They do not have the team concept. We would recommend that you continue your search for persons of experience in managerial ability and proven capacity.

Simon Peter - Is emotionally unstable and given to fits of temper.

Andrew - Has absolutely no qualities of leadership.

James - These two brothers place personal interest above company loyalty.

Thomas - Demonstrates a questioning attitude that would tend to undermine morale.

Matthew - has been blacklisted by the Greater Jerusalem Better Business Bureau.

James & Thaddeus - Both have definite radical leanings and they both registered a high score on the manic depressive scale.

One of the candidates, however, shows great potential. He is a man of ability and resourcefulness, meets people well, has a keen business mind and has contacts in high places. He is highly motivated, ambitious and responsible. We recommend Judas Iscariot as your controller and right-hand man. All of the other profiles are self-explanatory.

We wish you success in your new venture.

The Lord sees not as man sees.

God's ways are not our ways and He doesn't see people in the way that we do. We are so quick to judge! Would we have chosen Jonah or Samson or even Timothy who was so often ill?

Paul presses this lesson home in his letter to the Corinthians: 'Think of what you were when you were called. Not many of you were wise by human standards; not many were influential; not many were of noble birth...'

But God had chosen them!

Have you noticed how often staggering changes in history have been accomplished by the unlikely people? We all know about Florence Nightingale fighting for the right to become a doctor, when that option was only for men. Ghandi, that little spindly-legged man who led a huge nation to independence, and have you seen the film, 'Schindler's List'? If not, watch it! It's a wonderful story of a German officer in the Nazi hierarchy who rescued hundreds of Jews from the holocaust.

God has created each of us with an amazing potential to achieve and, with His enabling, to overcome what we see as our lack of ability. Paul again, in his letter to Timothy: 'I thank Jesus Christ our Lord, who has given me strength, that he considered me faithful, appointing me to His service.' And think what he had to cope with!

Oswald Chambers gives us good advice: 'Don't seek to

be strong; seek to be united with Jesus who makes us strong.' Paul was certain that he could do everything with God's strength. We mustn't back away from serving God because we feel inadequate. He has promised that when we feel weak, He is strong; in fact, His ability is shown best when we are at our lowest. Have you ever thought what that really means? The less capable we are, the more it will become evident that God is doing the work. So we have no excuse.

We all wish we could do great things for God but He is saying that He can do great things through us. We only have to willing and available.

There's a verse in Daniel which says: 'The people that know their God shall be strong and do exploits'. What's an 'exploit'? it is something extraordinary and unexpected. The secret is to know our God. That's what we have to work at, and He alone knows where that will lead.

Charles Price has written an excellent book entitled, *'Stop trying to live for Jesus, - let Him live through you.'* Very good advice. Let's follow it!